ADVANCED TYPE PROGRAMMING

FOR ANGULAR DEVELOPERS

OLIVER LUCAS JR

TABLE OF CONTENTS

Chapter 1

Chapter 2

Chapter 3

Chapter 4

Chapter 5

Chapter 6

Chapter 7

Chapter 8

Chapter 9

Preface

Welcome to the world of advanced TypeScript programming for Angular developers! This book is your guide to mastering the intricate dance between TypeScript and Angular, unlocking the true potential of this powerful combination.

As Angular applications grow in complexity, so does the need for robust, type-safe, and maintainable code. TypeScript, with its static typing and rich features, empowers you to build scalable Angular applications with confidence. This book delves deep into the synergy between TypeScript and Angular, equipping you with the knowledge and skills to tackle even the most challenging projects.

Who is this book for?

This book is tailored for Angular developers who possess a good working knowledge of TypeScript and are eager to elevate their skills to new heights. Whether you're building enterprise-level applications, crafting intricate user interfaces, or striving for architectural excellence, this book will be your companion on the journey to becoming a true TypeScript aficionado in the Angular realm.

What will you learn?

Within these pages, you'll embark on a comprehensive exploration of advanced TypeScript concepts and their practical applications in Angular development. You'll discover how to:

Master TypeScript's type system, wielding interfaces, generics, and advanced types to craft elegant and robust code.

Build reusable and type-safe Angular components, directives, and services that adapt seamlessly to diverse scenarios.

Harness the power of reactive programming with RxJS, managing asynchronous operations and data streams with finesse.

Construct complex forms with reactive forms and custom validators, ensuring data integrity and a smooth user experience.

Implement state management solutions with NgRx, architecting scalable applications with centralized and predictable state.

Optimize your Angular applications for peak performance, leveraging techniques like AOT compilation, lazy loading, and efficient change detection.

Write effective unit and end-to-end tests, ensuring code quality and reducing bugs.

Deploy your Angular applications to various platforms, from traditional web hosting to serverless functions and cloud environments.

How is this book structured?

This book is carefully structured to guide you through a progressive learning journey. We begin with a refresher on fundamental TypeScript concepts, laying a solid foundation for the advanced topics that follow. Each chapter builds upon the previous ones, introducing new concepts and techniques with clear explanations, practical examples, and real-world use cases.

Why this book?

This book is more than just a collection of code snippets and tutorials; it's a deep dive into the "why" behind the code. We'll explore the design patterns, best practices, and architectural considerations that underpin advanced TypeScript programming in Angular. By understanding the underlying principles, you'll be able to make informed decisions and write code that is not only functional but also elegant, maintainable, and scalable.

Join the journey!

We invite you to embark on this exciting journey into the world of advanced TypeScript programming for Angular developers. With dedication and a thirst for knowledge, you'll emerge from this experience equipped with the skills and confidence to tackle any Angular project with TypeScript as your trusted ally.

Chapter 1

TypeScript Fundamentals Refresher

1.1Types, Interfaces, Classes, Generics

Types

In the realm of TypeScript, understanding *types* is paramount. They are the bedrock upon which we build robust and reliable applications. Think of types as the labels we attach to data, informing the TypeScript compiler about the kind of values a variable can hold. This enables the compiler to act as a vigilant guardian, catching potential errors before they wreak havoc during runtime.

Basic Types

TypeScript offers a rich set of built-in types, mirroring the fundamental data types you encounter in programming. Let's explore these essential building blocks:

number: This type encompasses all numeric values, whether they are whole numbers (integers) or numbers with decimal points (floating-point numbers).

TypeScript

```
let age: number = 30;          // An integer
let price: number = 9.99;              // A
floating-point number
```

```
let temperature: number = -5;      // A negative
integer
```

string: Strings are sequences of characters, typically used to represent text. In TypeScript, you can enclose strings in either single (') or double (") quotes.

TypeScript

```
let name: string = "Alice";
let greeting: string = 'Hello, world!';
let message: string = `The value is ${age}`;   //
Template literals
```

boolean: This type represents the logical values true or false, often used for conditional statements and flags.

TypeScript

```
let isLoggedIn: boolean = true;
let isActive: boolean = false;
let isAdult: boolean = age >= 18;
```

`null`: While seemingly simple, `null` represents the intentional absence of a value. It signifies that a variable has been explicitly assigned the value of "nothing."

TypeScript

```
let user: null = null;  // Indicates that the 'user' is currently not assigned
```

`undefined`: In contrast to `null`, `undefined` indicates that a variable has not been assigned any value at all. It's the default state of a variable before you give it a value.

TypeScript

```
let city: undefined;   // 'city' has no value assigned yet
```

`symbol`: Symbols introduce a unique and immutable data type. They are often used to create unique identifiers within your code.

TypeScript

```
const uniqueId: symbol = Symbol("id");   // Creates a unique symbol
```

`bigint`: For those dealing with extremely large numbers that exceed the limits of regular numbers, TypeScript provides the `bigint` type. These are arbitrary-precision integers, allowing you to represent values of any size.

TypeScript

```
let        bigNumber:        bigint       =
12345678901234567890123456789  0n;   //   The   'n'
suffix denotes a bigint
```

1.2 Key TypeScript features relevant to Angular

Key TypeScript Features for Angular

While we'll delve deeper into these concepts in later chapters, let's take a moment to introduce some key TypeScript features that play a crucial role in Angular development:

Decorators: Think of decorators as special functions that add metadata to classes, methods, or properties.[1] They act like annotations, providing additional information about the code they decorate.[2] In Angular, decorators are extensively used to define components, modules, and services.[3] For example, the `@Component` decorator transforms a plain TypeScript class into an Angular component, specifying its template, styles, and selector.

TypeScript

```
@Component({
  selector: 'app-my-component',
  template: '<h1>Hello, {{ name }}!</h1>',
})
export class MyComponent {
  name = 'World';
}
```

Modules: Modules are a powerful tool for organizing your code into logical units.[4] They help you manage dependencies and keep your codebase clean and maintainable.[5] In Angular, modules are essential for structuring your application.[6] You'll use the @NgModule decorator to define modules, specifying the components, directives, and pipes that belong to them.

TypeScript

```
@NgModule({
  declarations: [AppComponent, MyComponent],
  imports: [BrowserModule],
  bootstrap: [AppComponent],
})
export class AppModule {}
```

Type Assertions: Sometimes, you might know the type of a value better than the TypeScript compiler does. In these cases, you can use type assertions to tell the compiler to treat a value as a specific type.[7] This can be particularly useful when working with

Angular's template system, where the compiler might not have enough information to infer the types of variables.

TypeScript

```
const                    element                    =
document.getElementById('my-element')              as
HTMLDivElement;
// Now you can access properties and methods
specific to HTMLDivElement
element.textContent = 'Hello!';
```

These TypeScript features are fundamental to Angular development. They contribute to the framework's structure, organization, and type safety. As you progress through this book, you'll gain a deeper understanding of how these features work together to create robust and maintainable Angular applications.

1.3 Setting up a TypeScript development environment

Excellent choice! Guiding your readers through setting up their TypeScript development environment is a practical and helpful way to start. Here's a draft of that section, focusing on clarity and ease of following:

Setting up a TypeScript Development Environment

Before you embark on your TypeScript coding journey, you need to prepare your development environment. This involves installing the necessary tools and configuring them correctly. Here's a step-by-step guide to get you started:

Install Node.js and npm:

Head over to the official Node.js website (https://nodejs.org) and download the installer for your operating system (Windows, macOS, or Linux).

Run the installer and follow the on-screen instructions. This[1] will install both Node.js and npm (the Node Package Manager), which is essential for managing JavaScript packages.

To verify the installation, open your terminal or command prompt and type `node -v` and `npm -v`. You should see the installed versions of Node.js and npm.[2]

Initialize a TypeScript project:

Open your terminal and navigate to the directory where you want to create your project.

Run the following command to initialize a new Node.js project:[3]

Bash

```
npm init -y
```

This will create a `package.json` file in your project directory, which will store information about your project and its dependencies.[4]

Next, install TypeScript as a development dependency using npm:

Bash

```bash
npm install --save-dev typescript
```

Create a tsconfig.json file:

In your project directory, create a file named `tsconfig.json`. This file contains various settings for the TypeScript compiler.

You can start with a basic configuration like this:

JSON

```json
{
  "compilerOptions": {
    "target": "es5",
    "module": "commonjs",
    "outDir": "./dist",
    "strict": true
  }
}
```

This configuration tells the compiler to:

Target ES5 for compatibility with older browsers.

Use CommonJS modules.

Output compiled JavaScript files to the `dist` directory.

Enable strict type checking.

Write your first TypeScript code:

Create a new file named `index.ts` (or any name you prefer with a `.ts` extension) in your project directory.

Add some TypeScript code to the file:

TypeScript

```typescript
function greet(name: string): string {
   return `Hello, ${name}!`;
}

console.log(greet('World'));
```

Compile your TypeScript code:

In your terminal, run the following command tocompile your TypeScript code:

Bash

```
npx tsc
```

This will generate a `index.js` file in the `dist` directory, containing the compiled JavaScript code.

Run your code:

In your terminal, navigate to the `dist` directory and run the compiled JavaScript file using Node.js:

Bash

```
node index.js
```

You should see the output "Hello, World!" in your terminal.

Congratulations! You have successfully set up a TypeScript development environment and run your first TypeScript code.

Chapter 2

Deep Dive into Angular's Type System

2.1 Understanding Angular's use of decorators, modules, and components

Deep Dive into Angular's Type System

Angular leverages TypeScript's type system to create a robust and maintainable framework. Understanding how Angular uses decorators, modules, and components, along with their interplay with TypeScript, is crucial for building sophisticated applications.

Decorators: The Metadata Magic

Decorators are a powerful TypeScript feature that Angular uses extensively. They are special functions that attach metadata to classes, properties, or methods. This metadata provides Angular with crucial information about how different parts of your application should behave.

`@Component`: This decorator is fundamental to Angular. It transforms a plain TypeScript class into an Angular component. The `@Component` decorator accepts an object with various properties, including:

`selector`: A CSS selector that tells Angular where to insert the component in the DOM.

`template` or `templateUrl`: Specifies the HTML template for the component's view.

`styles` or `styleUrls`: Defines the CSS styles for the component.

TypeScript

```
@Component({
  selector: 'app-my-component',
  template: '<h1>Hello, {{ name }}!</h1>',
})
export class MyComponent {
  name = 'World';
}
```

`@NgModule`: This decorator defines an Angular module, which is a container for a group of related components, services, and other code. Modules help organize your application and manage dependencies.

TypeScript

```
@NgModule({
  declarations: [AppComponent, MyComponent],
  imports: [BrowserModule],
  bootstrap: [AppComponent],
})
export class AppModule []
```

`@Injectable`: This decorator marks a class as an injectable service. Services are used to encapsulate reusable logic and data that can be shared across components.

TypeScript

```typescript
@Injectable({ providedIn: 'root' })
export class MyService {
  getData() {
    // ... service logic ...
  }
}
```

Modules: Organizing Your Application

Modules are the building blocks of an Angular application. They encapsulate components, services, and other code into cohesive units. The `@NgModule` decorator defines a module and its properties:

`declarations`: An array of components, directives, and pipes that belong to this module.

`imports`: An array of other modules that this module depends on.

`exports`: An array of components, directives, and pipes that this module makes available to other modules.

`providers`: An array of services that this module provides.

`bootstrap`: The root component that Angular should bootstrap when launching the application.

Components: Building Blocks of the UI

Components are the fundamental UI building blocks in Angular. They combine an HTML template with a TypeScript class to create reusable UI elements.

Template: The template defines the component's view using HTML. It can include data bindings, directives, and other Angular template syntax.

Class: The class contains the component's logic, including properties, methods, and lifecycle hooks. It interacts with the template through data binding and event handling.

TypeScript's Role

TypeScript plays a crucial role in making Angular's decorators, modules, and components type-safe and maintainable.

Type Checking: TypeScript ensures that data flows correctly between components and services, catching potential errors early on.

Code Completion and Navigation: TypeScript's type information enables powerful code completion and navigation features in your IDE, improving developer productivity.

Refactoring: TypeScript makes refactoring safer and easier, as the compiler can identify potential issues caused by code changes.

2.2 Advanced component architecture with TypeScript (e.g., lifecycle hooks, change detection)

Advanced Component Architecture with TypeScript

Angular components are more than just UI building blocks; they have a lifecycle managed by the framework. Understanding this lifecycle and how to interact with it using lifecycle hooks is key to building sophisticated Angular applications. TypeScript plays a crucial role in defining and interacting with these lifecycle events.

Lifecycle Hooks

Angular components go through a series of stages from creation to destruction. Lifecycle hooks are special methods that allow you to tap into these stages and execute code at specific points. Here are some of the key lifecycle hooks:

`ngOnInit()`: This hook is called once, after the component's inputs have been initialized. It's a good place to perform initialization logic, such as fetching data from a server or setting up subscriptions.

TypeScript

```typescript
ngOnInit(): void {
  this.myService.getData().subscribe(data => {
    this.items = data;
  });
}
```

`ngOnChanges()`: This hook is called whenever one or more of the component's input properties change. It receives a `SimpleChanges` object that contains information about the previous and current values of the changed properties.

TypeScript

```typescript
ngOnChanges(changes: SimpleChanges): void {
```

```
if (changes['myInputProperty']) {
    console.log('My input property changed!',
changes['myInputProperty']);
  }
}
```

`ngOnDestroy()`: This hook is called just before the component is destroyed. It's a good place to clean up resources, such as unsubscribing from observables[1] or clearing timers, to prevent memory leaks.

TypeScript

```
ngOnDestroy(): void {
  this.dataSubscription.unsubscribe();
}
```

`ngDoCheck()`: This hook is called during every change detection cycle. It allows you to implement custom change detection logic, but use it with caution as it can impact performance if not implemented efficiently.

Change Detection

Change detection is the mechanism Angular uses to keep the view synchronized with the component's data. When a component's data changes, Angular detects those changes and updates the view accordingly.

Default Change Detection: By default, Angular uses a change detection strategy called `ChangeDetectionStrategy.Default`. This strategy checks all components in the component tree for changes whenever an event occurs, such as a user interaction or an asynchronous operation.

`OnPush` **Change Detection:** For performance optimization, you can use the `ChangeDetectionStrategy.OnPush` strategy. This strategy tells Angular to only check a component for changes when its inputs change or when an event is emitted from within the component.

TypeScript

```typescript
@Component({
  // ...
  changeDetection: ChangeDetectionStrategy.OnPush
})
export class MyComponent {
  // ...
}
```

TypeScript and Change Detection

TypeScript plays a vital role in making change detection more efficient and predictable:

Immutability: Using immutable data structures with `OnPush` change detection can significantly improve performance. When an input property receives a new immutable object, Angular can quickly detect the change and update the view without having to deeply compare the object's properties.

Interfaces and Types: Defining clear interfaces and types for your component's inputs and outputs helps ensure that data flows correctly and that change detection operates as expected.

2.3 Dependency injection and its role in type safety

Dependency Injection and Its Role in Type Safety

Dependency Injection is a design pattern where a class receives its dependencies from an external source rather than creating them itself.[2] In Angular, this "external source" is the framework's powerful dependency injection system.[3] This approach promotes loose coupling, modularity, and testability, and TypeScript enhances these benefits with type safety.[4]

How Dependency Injection Works in Angular

Declare Dependencies: In an Angular component or service, you declare dependencies in the constructor.[5] This signals to Angular that the class needs these dependencies to function.

TypeScript

```
constructor(private myService: MyService) { }
```

Provide Dependencies: You tell Angular how to provide these dependencies.[6] This is often done using the providers array in an `@NgModule` or by using the `providedIn` property in an `@Injectable` decorator.

TypeScript

```typescript
@NgModule({
  // ...
  providers: [MyService],
  // ...
})
export class AppModule { }

// Or, in the service itself:

@Injectable({ providedIn: 'root' })
export class MyService {
  // ...
}
```

Angular Injects Dependencies: When Angular creates a new instance of a component or service, it looks at the constructor parameters to identify the dependencies.[7] It then resolves these dependencies from its injector and provides them to the class.

Benefits of Dependency Injection

Loose Coupling: Classes are not tightly bound to their dependencies, making them more flexible and easier to maintain.[8]

Modularity: DI encourages breaking down applications into smaller, more manageable modules.[9]

Testability: It's easier to write unit tests for classes that use DI because you can easily mock or stub their dependencies.[10]

Reusability: Dependencies can be easily reused across different parts of the application.[11]

Type Safety with Dependency Injection

TypeScript enhances Angular's DI system by adding type safety.[12]

Compile-Time Checks: When you declare dependencies with their types in the constructor, TypeScript ensures that the injected dependencies match the expected types. This helps catch errors early in the development process.

Code Completion and Navigation: Your IDE can provide accurate code completion and navigation suggestions because it understands the types of the injected dependencies.

Refactoring: Refactoring becomes safer and more efficient because TypeScript can help identify potential type-related issues caused by code changes.

Example

TypeScript

```typescript
// my.service.ts
@Injectable({ providedIn: 'root' })
export class MyService {
  getData(): string {
    return 'Data from MyService';
  }
}

// my.component.ts
@Component({
```

```
  // ...
})
export class MyComponent {
  data: string;

  constructor(private myService: MyService) {
    this.data = this.myService.getData();
  }
}
```

In this example, MyComponent depends on MyService. By declaring myService with its type in the constructor, we ensure type safety. TypeScript will verify that the injected service matches the MyService type, and your IDE will provide code completion for myService methods.

Chapter 3

Mastering TypeScript Generics in Angular

3.1 Building reusable and type-safe components with generics

Mastering TypeScript Generics in Angular

Generics are a powerful tool in TypeScript that allow you to write code that can work with a variety of types without sacrificing type safety. This is particularly valuable in Angular when building reusable components. Imagine creating a single component that can handle different data types seamlessly, adapting to various use cases throughout your application. That's the magic of generics!

Building Reusable Components with Generics

Let's say you need a component to display a list of items. This list could contain anything: products, users, articles, etc. Instead of creating separate components for each type of list, you can create a single generic list component.

TypeScript

```typescript
@Component({
  selector: 'app-generic-list',
  template: `
    <ul>
        <li *ngFor="let item of items">{{ item |
json }}</li>
    </ul>
```

```
})
export class GenericListComponent<T> {
  @Input() items: T[] = [];
}
```

In this example, `GenericListComponent` has a type parameter `T`. This means it can work with any type of item. The `items` input is now an array of type `T`, allowing you to pass in arrays of numbers, strings, objects, or any other type.

Using the Generic Component

You can then use this generic component with different types:

TypeScript

```
// In your parent component's template:
<app-generic-list
[items]="numbers"></app-generic-list>
<app-generic-list
[items]="users"></app-generic-list>

// In your parent component's class:
numbers: number[] = [1, 2, 3];
users: { name: string, age: number }[] = [
  { name: 'Alice', age: 30 },
  { name: 'Bob', age: 25 },
];
```

Benefits of Generic Components

Reusability: Write once, use anywhere! A single generic component can adapt to different data types, reducing code duplication.

Type Safety: Even with the flexibility of generics, you retain strong type checking. The compiler ensures that the data you pass to the component matches the expected type.

Maintainability: Updates and bug fixes to the generic component automatically apply to all its uses.

Beyond Basic Lists

Generics are not limited to simple lists. You can use them to create reusable components for various purposes, such as:

Generic Forms: Create forms that can handle different data models.

Generic Modals: Build modals that can display different content types.

Generic Data Tables: Design tables that can work with various data structures.

3.2 Creating custom generic directives and services

You're thinking like a true TypeScript pro! Generics aren't just for components; they can significantly enhance the flexibility and reusability of your directives and services as well. Let's explore how to create custom generic directives and services in Angular.

Creating Custom Generic Directives

Directives allow you to extend the functionality of HTML elements. By using generics, you can create directives that adapt to different data types and scenarios.

Example: A Generic Validation Directive

Imagine you need a directive to validate input fields based on a specific condition. This condition might vary depending on the type of data being input. A generic directive can handle this beautifully.

TypeScript

```typescript
@Directive({
  selector: '[appGenericValidator]',
})
export class GenericValidatorDirective<T> {
    @Input() appGenericValidator: (value: T) =>
boolean;
  @Input() validationMessage: string;

    constructor(private el: ElementRef, private
renderer: Renderer2) {}

  @HostListener('blur')
  onBlur() {
    const value: T = this.el.nativeElement.value;
    if (!this.appGenericValidator(value)) {

this.renderer.setProperty(this.el.nativeElement,
'title', this.validationMessage);
    } else {

this.renderer.removeAttribute(this.el.nativeEleme
nt, 'title');
    }
```

```
    }
}
```

In this example, `GenericValidatorDirective` takes a type parameter `T` representing the input value's type. The `appGenericValidator` input accepts a validation function that takes a value of type `T` and returns a boolean indicating whether the value is valid.

Using the Directive

HTML

```
<input          type="text"          [(ngModel)]="name"
appGenericValidator="validateName"
validationMessage="Name    must    be    at    least    3
characters long">

<input          type="number"          [(ngModel)]="age"
appGenericValidator="validateAge"
validationMessage="Age must be 18 or older">
```

TypeScript

```typescript
// In your component:
validateName(name: string): boolean {
  return name.length >= 3;
}

validateAge(age: number): boolean {
  return age >= 18;
}
```

This directive can now be used to validate any input type by providing the appropriate validation function.

Creating Custom Generic Services

Services often handle data manipulation or interactions with external APIs. Generics can make your services more versatile and type-safe.

Example: A Generic Data Service

Let's say you need a service to fetch data from different endpoints of an API. A generic service can handle this with type safety.

TypeScript

```typescript
@Injectable({ providedIn: 'root' })
export class GenericDataService<T> {
  constructor(private http: HttpClient) {}

  getData(url: string): Observable<T[]> {
    return this.http.get<T[]>(url);
  }
}
```

This `GenericDataService` can fetch data from any endpoint and return an `Observable` of the specified type `T`.

Using the Service

TypeScript

```typescript
// In your component:
```

```
constructor(private                 productService:
GenericDataService<Product>, private userService:
GenericDataService<User>) {}

ngOnInit() {

this.productService.getData('/api/products').subs
cribe(products => {
    // ...
  });


this.userService.getData('/api/users').subscribe(
users => {
    // ...
  });
}
```

By injecting `GenericDataService` with specific types (`Product` and `User`), you create strongly typed services that handle different data types.

Benefits of Generic Directives and Services

Reusability: Write less code and apply your directives and services to various scenarios.

Type Safety: Maintain strong typing even with increased flexibility.

Maintainability: Updates to generic directives or services benefit all their uses.

3.3 Advanced use cases: generic factories, constraints, and conditional types

Advanced Use Cases: Generic Factories, Constraints, and Conditional Types

Generic Factories

Generic factories are functions that create objects based on a provided type.[2] This can be extremely useful when you need to create objects of different types with a consistent structure.

TypeScript

```typescript
function createInstance<T>(c: { new (): T }): T {
  return new c();
}
```

This `createInstance` function takes a class constructor as an argument and returns a new instance of that class.

Example Usage

TypeScript

```typescript
class Product {
  name: string;
  price: number;
}

class User {
  name: string;
  email: string;
}
```

```
const product = createInstance<Product>(Product);
 const user = createInstance<User>(User);
```

This allows you to create instances of different classes without repeating the `new` keyword and while maintaining type safety.

Generic Constraints

Generic constraints limit the types that can be used with a generic type parameter.[3] This is useful when you need to ensure that a type has certain properties or methods.

TypeScript

```
function logLength<T extends { length: number }>(value: T): void {
  console.log(value.length);
}
```

In this example, the `logLength` function only accepts types that have a `length` property.

Conditional Types

Conditional types allow you to create types that depend on a condition.[4] This enables you to express complex type relationships.[5]

TypeScript

```
type IsNumber<T> = T extends number ? 'yes' : 'no';

type Type1 = IsNumber<number>;  // 'yes'
```

```
type Type2 = IsNumber<string>;    // 'no'
```

Here, `IsNumber<T>` checks if the type `T` is a number. If it is, the type resolves to `'yes'`, otherwise `'no'`.

Combining Concepts: A Practical Example

Let's combine these concepts to create a generic factory with constraints and conditional types.

TypeScript

```
type HasNameProperty<T> = T extends { name:
string } ? T : never;

function createNamedInstance<T>(c: { new (): T
}): HasNameProperty<T> {
  const instance = new c();
  if ('name' in instance) {
    return instance as HasNameProperty<T>;
  }
  return null;
}
```

This `createNamedInstance` function:

Uses a constraint to ensure that the provided class has a `name` property.

Uses a conditional type `HasNameProperty` to refine the return type based on whether the created instance has a `name` property.

3.3 Advanced use cases: generic factories, constraints, and conditional types

Advanced Use Cases: Generic Factories, Constraints, and Conditional Types

Generic Factories

Imagine a scenario where you need to create objects of different classes, but these classes share a similar structure or set of properties. Instead of writing repetitive object creation code, you can employ a generic factory function.[1] This function acts as a blueprint, taking a class constructor as an argument and returning a new instance of that class.[2]

TypeScript

```
function createInstance<T>(c: { new (): T }): T {
  return new c();
}
```

In this example, `createInstance` is our generic factory. The type parameter `T` represents the type of object to be created. The constraint `{ new (): T }` ensures that the argument `c` is a class constructor that can be invoked with `new` to create an object of type `T`.

Example Usage

TypeScript

```
class Product {
  name: string;
  price: number;
```

```
  constructor() {
    this.name = '';
    this.price = 0;
  }
}

class User {
  name: string;
  email: string;

  constructor() {
    this.name = '';
    this.email = '';
  }
}

const product = createInstance<Product>(Product);
 const user = createInstance<User>(User);
```

This demonstrates how `createInstance` can be used to create instances of both `Product` and `User` classes without duplicating the `new` keyword, all while maintaining type safety.

Generic Constraints

Generic constraints allow you to restrict the types that can be used with a generic type parameter.[3] This is invaluable when you need to ensure that a type possesses specific properties or methods.

TypeScript

```
function logLength<T extends { length: number }>(value: T): void {
  console.log(value.length);
}
```

In this example, `logLength` only accepts types that have a `length` property. This constraint ensures that you can safely access the `length` property of the `value` argument without encountering runtime errors.

Conditional Types

Conditional types introduce a level of dynamism to your type definitions.[4] They allow you to create types that change based on a condition, enabling you to express complex type relationships.

TypeScript

```typescript
type IsNumber<T> = T extends number ? 'yes' : 'no';

type Type1 = IsNumber<number>;  // 'yes'
type Type2 = IsNumber<string>;  // 'no'
```

Here, `IsNumber<T>` checks if the type `T` extends `number`. If it does, the type resolves to `'yes'`, otherwise `'no'`. This allows you to perform type-level checks and create types that adapt based on the outcome.

Combining Concepts: A Practical Example

Let's combine these concepts to create a generic factory with constraints and conditional types.

TypeScript

```typescript
type HasNameProperty<T> = T extends { name: string } ? T : never;
```

```
function createNamedInstance<T>(c: { new (): T
}): HasNameProperty<T> {
  const instance = new c();
  if ('name' in instance) {
    return instance as HasNameProperty<T>;
  }
  return null;
}
```

This `createNamedInstance` function:

Uses a constraint (`{ new (): T }`) to ensure that the provided argument is a class constructor.

Uses a conditional type `HasNameProperty` to refine the return type. If the created instance has a `name` property, the return type is `T`; otherwise, it's `never`, indicating that the function will never return a value of that type.

Chapter 4

Reactive Programming with RxJS and TypeScript

4.1 Observables, Subjects, and Operators in RxJS

Reactive Programming with RxJS and TypeScript

RxJS (Reactive Extensions for JavaScript) is a library that brings the principles of reactive programming to JavaScript. It provides a set of tools for working with asynchronous data streams, making it easier to handle events, user input, network requests, and more. TypeScript further enhances RxJS by adding type safety to your reactive code.

Observables: The Foundation

Observables are the core of RxJS. They represent a stream of values that can be emitted over time. Think of an Observable as a pipeline through which data flows. You can "subscribe" to an Observable to receive these values as they are emitted.

TypeScript

```typescript
import { Observable } from 'rxjs';

const myObservable = new Observable<number>(observer => {
  observer.next(1);
  observer.next(2);
  setTimeout(() => {
    observer.next(3);
```

```
    observer.complete();
  }, 1000);
});

myObservable.subscribe({
  next: (value) => console.log('Received value:',
value),
    error:   (err)   =>   console.error('Received
error:', err),
    complete:   ()   =>   console.log('Observable
completed'),
});
```

Subjects: The Multicasters

Subjects are a special type of Observable that allow you to "push" values into the stream. They act as both an Observable and an Observer. This means you can subscribe to a Subject to receive values, and you can also use the next() method to emit values into the Subject.

TypeScript

```
import { Subject } from 'rxjs';

const mySubject = new Subject<string>();

mySubject.subscribe(value                           =>
console.log('Observer 1:', value));
mySubject.subscribe(value                           =>
console.log('Observer 2:', value));

mySubject.next('Hello!');[1]   //   Both   observers
receive 'Hello!'
```

Operators: The Transformers

Operators are functions that allow you to manipulate and transform the values emitted by an Observable. RxJS provides a vast collection of operators for filtering, mapping, combining, and transforming data streams.

TypeScript

```
import { from } from 'rxjs';
import { map, filter } from 'rxjs/operators';

const numbers = from([1, 2, 3, 4, 5]);

const evenNumbers = numbers.pipe(
  filter(x => x % 2 === 0),
  map(x => x * 2)
);

evenNumbers.subscribe(value                            =>
console.log(value)); // Outputs 4, 8
```

TypeScript and RxJS

TypeScript adds type safety to your RxJS code by allowing you to specify the types of values emitted by Observables and Subjects. This helps catch errors early and improves code readability.

TypeScript

```
const myObservable: Observable<string> = // ...;
const mySubject: Subject<number> = // ...;
```

By understanding and effectively using Observables, Subjects, and Operators in RxJS with TypeScript, you can write more efficient, readable, and maintainable code for handling asynchronous operations and managing complex data flows in your Angular applications.

4.2 Strong typing with RxJS: defining custom operators and types

You're spot on! Strong typing is one of the key benefits TypeScript brings to RxJS. By defining custom operators and types, you can make your reactive code even more robust, readable, and maintainable. Let's dive in!

Strong Typing with RxJS: Custom Operators and Types

TypeScript allows you to define custom operators that are not only reusable but also type-safe. This ensures that your operators work correctly with the data flowing through your Observables.

Defining a Custom Operator

Here's an example of a custom operator that doubles the values emitted by an Observable:

TypeScript

```typescript
import { MonoTypeOperatorFunction, Observable } from 'rxjs';
import { map } from 'rxjs/operators';

function double<T extends number>(): MonoTypeOperatorFunction<T> {
  return (source: Observable<T>) => source.pipe(
    map(value => value * 2)
  );
```

}

In this example:

We define a function `double` that takes no arguments and returns a `MonoTypeOperatorFunction<T>`. This type represents an operator that takes an Observable of type `T` and returns an Observable of the same type.

The constraint `T extends number` ensures that the operator only works with Observables that emit numbers.

Inside the function, we use the `pipe` method to combine the `map` operator, which multiplies each value by 2.

Using the Custom Operator

TypeScript

```typescript
import { of } from 'rxjs';

const numbers$ = of(1, 2, 3);

const doubledNumbers$ = numbers$.pipe(double());

doubledNumbers$.subscribe(value =>
console.log(value)); // Outputs 2, 4, 6
```

Defining Custom Types

You can also define custom types to represent the data flowing through your Observables. This can improve code readability and maintainability.

TypeScript

```
interface User {
  name: string;
  age: number;
}

const users$: Observable<User[]> = // ...;
```

Benefits of Strong Typing

Early Error Detection: TypeScript can catch type errors during development, preventing runtime surprises.

Improved Code Readability: Clear type annotations make it easier to understand the data flowing through your Observables.

Enhanced Code Maintainability: Refactoring and modifying your code becomes safer with type checking.

Better Developer Experience: IDEs can provide better code completion and suggestions with strong typing.

By combining the power of RxJS with TypeScript's strong typing capabilities, you can create highly robust and maintainable reactive code in your Angular applications.

4.3 Practical examples in Angular: handling asynchronous operations, data streams

Practical Examples in Angular

1. Handling HTTP Requests

One of the most common use cases for RxJS in Angular is handling HTTP requests. Angular's `HttpClient` returns Observables, allowing you to easily manage asynchronous data fetching.

TypeScript

```typescript
import { HttpClient } from '@angular/common/http';
import { Component } from '@angular/core';

interface Product {
  id: number;
  name: string;
  price: number;
}

@Component({
  selector: 'app-product-list',
  template: `
    <ul>
        <li *ngFor="let product of products$ | async">
        {{ product.name }} - ${{ product.price }}
      </li>
    </ul>
  `,
})
export class ProductListComponent {
  products$: Observable<Product[]>;

  constructor(private http: HttpClient) {
                      this.products$ =
this.http.get<Product[]>('/api/products');
  }
}
```

In this example:

We inject the `HttpClient` service.

We use `http.get<Product[]>('/api/products')` to fetch products from an API. This returns an `Observable<Product[]>`.

We use the `async` pipe in the template to subscribe to the `products$` Observable and display the products.

2. User Input with Reactive Forms

RxJS is often used with Angular's reactive forms to handle user input as a stream of values.

TypeScript

```
import { Component } from '@angular/core';
import { FormControl } from '@angular/forms';
import { debounceTime, distinctUntilChanged,
switchMap } from 'rxjs/operators';[1]

@Component({
  selector: 'app-search',
  template: `
                              <input      type="text"
[formControl]="searchInput">[2]
    <ul>
      <li *ngFor="let result of searchResults$ |
async">
        {{ result }}
      </li>
    </ul>
  `
})
export class[3] SearchComponent {
  searchInput = new FormControl('');
  searchResults$: Observable<string[]>;

  constructor() {
```

```
                    this.searchResults$      =
this.searchInput.valueChanges.pipe(
      debounceTime(300),4
      distinctUntilChanged(),
                    switchMap(searchTerm     =>
this.search(searchTerm))
    );
  }

  search(term: string): Observable<string[]> {
    // Simulate an API call
    return of([`Result 1 for ${term}`, `Result 2
for ${term}`]);
  }
}
```

In this example:

We use `valueChanges` to get an Observable of the search input's value.

We use `debounceTime` to only emit values after a pause in typing.

We use `distinctUntilChanged` to only emit when the value actually changes.

We use `switchMap` to cancel previous requests and make a new search API call.

3. Real-time Updates with WebSockets

RxJS is excellent for handling real-time updates from WebSockets.

TypeScript

```
import { webSocket, WebSocketSubject } from
'rxjs/webSocket';

const                    subject                    =
webSocket('wss://echo.websocket.org');

subject.subscribe(
  msg => console.log('message received: ' + msg),
  err => console.log(err),
  () => console.log('complete')
);

subject.next({ op: 'subscribe', channel: 'ticker'
});
```

In this example:

We use `webSocket` to create a `WebSocketSubject`.

We subscribe to the Subject to receive messages.

We use `subject.next()` to send messages through the WebSocket.

These are just a few examples of how RxJS can be used to handle asynchronous operations and data streams in Angular. With its powerful operators and TypeScript's type safety, RxJS provides a robust and elegant way to build reactive and responsive applications.

Chapter 5

Advanced Angular Forms with TypeScript

5.1 Building complex forms with reactive forms and strong typing

You're delving into a crucial aspect of Angular development! Reactive forms, combined with TypeScript's strong typing, offer a robust and maintainable way to handle complex forms. Let's explore how to build these forms effectively.

Building Complex Forms with Reactive Forms and Strong Typing

Angular's reactive forms provide a model-driven approach to handling forms. You define the structure of your form in your component's TypeScript code, giving you more control and flexibility. TypeScript enhances this approach by adding type safety, ensuring that your form data is always valid and predictable.

1. Defining the Form Model

Start by defining a TypeScript interface or class that represents the structure of your form data.

TypeScript

```typescript
interface User {
  firstName: string;
  lastName: string;
  email: string;
```

```
  address: {
    street: string;
    city: string;
    country: string;
  };
}
```

2. Creating the Form Group

Use Angular's `FormGroup` and `FormControl` classes to create a form group that mirrors your data model.

TypeScript

```
import { Component } from '@angular/core';
import { FormGroup, FormControl, Validators }
from '@angular/forms';

@Component({
  selector: 'app-user-form',
  templateUrl: './user-form.component.html',[1]
})
export class UserFormComponent {
  userForm[2] = new FormGroup({
            firstName:   new   FormControl('',
Validators.required),
              lastName:   new   FormControl('',
Validators.required),
                email:   new   FormControl('',
[Validators.required,[3] Validators.email]),
      address: new FormGroup({
        street: new FormControl(''),[4]
        city: new FormControl(''),
        country: new FormControl(''),
```

```
  }),
 });
}
```

3. Strong Typing the Form

To add strong typing, you can create a type alias for your form group.

TypeScript

```
type UserForm = FormGroup<{
   firstName: FormControl<string>;
   lastName: FormControl<string>;
   email: FormControl<string>;
   address: FormGroup<{
      street: FormControl<string>;
      city: FormControl<string>;
      country: FormControl<string>;
   }>;
}>;

userForm: UserForm = new FormGroup({
   // ... (same as before)
});
```

This ensures that your form group adheres to the defined structure and that you can access its controls with type safety.

4. Accessing Form Controls and Values

You can access individual form controls and their values using the get() method and the value property.

TypeScript

```typescript
get firstName() {
  return this.userForm.get('firstName');
}

onSubmit() {
  const formData: User = this.userForm.value;
  // ... submit the form data ...
}
```

5. Displaying the Form in the Template

Use Angular's form directives (formGroup, formControlName, etc.) to bind your form group to the template.

HTML

```html
<form                        [formGroup]="userForm"
(ngSubmit)="onSubmit()">
  <div formGroupName="address">
    </div>
  <button type="submit">Submit</button>
</form>
```

Benefits of Strong Typing

Compile-Time Validation: TypeScript checks your form structure and data types during development, preventing runtime errors.

Improved Code Readability: Clear type annotations make your form code easier to understand and maintain.

Enhanced Developer Experience: Your IDE can provide better code completion and suggestions with strong typing.

By combining reactive forms with TypeScript's strong typing, you can build complex forms that are robust, maintainable, and type-safe. This approach ensures that your forms handle data consistently and predictably, leading to a better user experience and fewer bugs.

5.2 Custom form controls and validators with type safety

Custom Form Controls and Validators with Type Safety

While Angular provides built-in form controls and validators, you might need to create your own to handle unique validation scenarios or implement custom behaviors. TypeScript ensures that these custom elements are type-safe and integrate seamlessly with your reactive forms.

1. Creating a Custom Form Control

Let's say you need a custom control to represent a percentage value, ensuring it always stays within the 0-100 range.

TypeScript

```typescript
import { FormControl } from '@angular/forms';

export class PercentageControl extends FormControl {
  constructor(value: number = 0) {
    super(value);
  }

  setValue(value: number, options?: any) {
    if (value < 0) {
      super.setValue(0, options);
    } else if (value > 100) {
```

```
      super.setValue(100, options);
    } else {
      super.setValue(value, options);
    }
  }
}
```

This `PercentageControl` extends the `FormControl` class and overrides the `setValue` method to enforce the percentage range.

2. Creating a Custom Validator

Now, let's create a custom validator to check if a password and confirm password fields match.

TypeScript

```
import { AbstractControl, ValidationErrors,
ValidatorFn } from '@angular/forms';

export                                function
passwordMatchValidator(passwordControlName:
string,   confirmPasswordControlName:   string):
ValidatorFn {
    return  (control:   AbstractControl):
ValidationErrors | null => {
        const    passwordControl    =
control.get(passwordControlName);
        const   confirmPasswordControl   =
control.get(confirmPasswordControlName);

        if   (passwordControl?.value   !==
confirmPasswordControl?.value) {
      return { passwordMismatch: true };
    }
```

```
    return null;
  };
}
```

This `passwordMatchValidator` function takes the names of the password and confirm password controls and returns a validator function. This function checks if the values of the two controls match and returns an error object if they don't.

3. Using Custom Controls and Validators

You can use your custom controls and validators in your form group.

TypeScript

```typescript
import { Component } from '@angular/core';
import { FormGroup, Validators } from '@angular/forms';
import { PercentageControl } from './percentage.control';
import { passwordMatchValidator } from './password-match.validator';

@Component({
  // ...
})
export class MyFormComponent {
  myForm = new FormGroup({
    percentage: new PercentageControl(50),
    password: new FormControl('', Validators.required),
    confirmPassword: new FormControl('', Validators.required),
```

```
                    },              {              validators:
passwordMatchValidator('password',[1]
'confirmPassword') });
}
```

Benefits of Strong Typing

Type Safety: TypeScript ensures that your custom controls and validators work with the correct data types.

Code Reusability: You can reuse your custom controls and validators across different forms.

Maintainability: Strong typing makes your code easier to understand and maintain.

By creating custom form controls and validators with TypeScript, you gain more control over your forms and ensure type safety throughout your application. This leads to more robust, maintainable, and user-friendly forms.

5.3 Dynamic form generation and validation

Dynamic Form Generation and Validation

Dynamic forms are essential when you don't know the exact structure of your form beforehand. This could be because:

The form fields depend on user input.

You're building a form builder application.

You're fetching form structure from an API.

1. Defining a Flexible Data Model

Since your form structure is dynamic, you need a flexible data model to represent it.

TypeScript

```typescript
interface Field {
    type: string; // e.g., 'text', 'number',
'select'
  label: string;
  name: string;
  options?: string[]; // For select fields
  required?: boolean;
}

interface FormDefinition {
  fields: Field[];
}
```

2. Generating Form Controls Dynamically

You can use a service to generate form controls based on your form definition.

TypeScript

```typescript
import { Injectable } from '@angular/core';
import { FormBuilder, FormGroup, Validators }
from '@angular/forms';
import { Field, FormDefinition } from
'./form.model';

@Injectable({ providedIn: 'root' })
export class DynamicFormService {
  constructor(private fb: FormBuilder) {}

    createForm(formDefinition: FormDefinition):
FormGroup {
    const formGroup = this.fb.group({});
```

```
    formDefinition.fields.forEach(field => {
      const validators = [];
      if (field.required) {
        validators.push(Validators.required);
      }
                    formGroup.addControl(field.name,
this.fb.control('', validators));
    });
    return formGroup;
  }
}
```

3. Building the Form Component

In your component, fetch the form definition and use the service to create the form group.

TypeScript

```
import { Component } from '@angular/core';
import { FormGroup } from '@angular/forms';
import      {      DynamicFormService      }      from
'./dynamic-form.service';
import { FormDefinition } from './form.model';

@Component({
  selector: 'app-dynamic-form',
  templateUrl: './dynamic-form.component.html',
})
export class DynamicFormComponent {
  formDefinition: FormDefinition = {
    fields: [
      // ... your dynamic field definitions ...
    ],
  };
```

```
form: FormGroup;

    constructor(private    dynamicFormService:
DynamicFormService) {
                   this.form        =
this.dynamicFormService.createForm(this.formDefin
ition);
  }
}
```

4. Rendering the Form in the Template

Use ngSwitch or similar techniques to render different field types based on the type property in your field definition.

HTML

```
<form [formGroup]="form">
         <div      *ngFor="let      field      of
formDefinition.fields">
    <div [ngSwitch]="field.type">
        <input *ngSwitchCase="'text'" type="text"
[formControlName]="field.name">
              <input    *ngSwitchCase="'number'"
type="number" [formControlName]="field.name">
       </div>
   </div>
   <button type="submit">Submit</button>
</form>
```

5. Dynamic Validation

You can add dynamic validation by using conditional validators or by adding/removing validators based on user input.

Benefits of Strong Typing

Type Safety: TypeScript ensures that your form controls and data adhere to the defined types, even with a dynamic structure.

Code Maintainability: Strong typing makes it easier to understand and maintain your dynamic form code.

Reduced Errors: TypeScript helps catch type-related errors during development, preventing runtime issues.

By combining dynamic form generation with TypeScript's type safety, you can build highly flexible and adaptable forms that are also robust and maintainable. This approach allows you to create forms that respond to user needs and external data while ensuring data integrity and a smooth user experience.

Chapter 6

State Management with NgRx and TypeScript

6.1 Introduction to NgRx: Store, Actions, Reducers, Selectors

Introduction to NgRx: Store, Actions, Reducers, Selectors

NgRx is a powerful state management library for Angular applications, inspired by Redux. It provides a centralized store to hold your application's state, along with mechanisms to update that state in a predictable and efficient manner. This leads to more maintainable and scalable applications, especially when dealing with complex data flows and interactions.

1. Store

The NgRx Store is a centralized, immutable data store that holds the entire state of your application. Think of it as a single source of truth for your data. Components can access and subscribe to the store to get the data they need, and they can dispatch actions to update the store.

2. Actions

Actions are plain JavaScript objects that describe an event or intention to modify the state. They have a `type` property that indicates the kind of action and an optional `payload` property to carry data.

TypeScript

```typescript
// Example action to add a product to a shopping
cart
const addProduct = createAction(
  '[Product List] Add Product',
  props<{ productId: number }>()
);
```

3. Reducers

Reducers are pure functions that take the current state and an action as input and return a new state. They are responsible for updating the[1] state in response to actions.

TypeScript

```typescript
// Example reducer for a shopping cart
function    cartReducer(state:    CartState    =
initialState, action: Action): CartState {
  switch (action.type) {
    case addProduct.type:
              return { ...state, products:
[...state.products, action.productId] };
    default:
      return state;
  }
}
```

4. Selectors

Selectors are functions that retrieve specific pieces of state from the store. They allow you to efficiently access the data your components need without having to deal with the entire state object.

TypeScript

```typescript
// Example selector to get the number of products
in the cart
const selectCartCount = createSelector(
  selectCartState,
  (state: CartState) => state.products.length
);
```

How NgRx Works

Dispatch an Action: A component dispatches an action to signal an intent to modify the state.

Reducer Updates State: The NgRx Store passes the action to the appropriate reducer.

New State: The reducer calculates the new state based on the action and the previous state.

Store Updates: The store updates its internal state with the new state returned by the reducer.

Selectors Retrieve Data: Components use selectors to retrieve the specific data they need from the updated state.

Components Update: Components that are subscribed to the store are notified of the state change and update their views accordingly.

Benefits of NgRx

Centralized State: Provides a single source of truth for your application's data.

Predictable State Changes: Actions and reducers make state changes predictable and easy to reason about.

Improved Performance: Selectors and change detection optimize data flow and updates.

Testability: Actions, reducers, and selectors are pure functions, making them easy to test.

Developer Tools: NgRx provides developer tools for debugging and inspecting state changes.

By understanding and effectively using NgRx, you can build robust and scalable Angular applications with well-managed state and improved performance.

6.2 Building type-safe NgRx applications

1. Define Strong Types for Your State

Start by defining clear and specific types for your application state using TypeScript interfaces or classes. This ensures that your state always adheres to a predefined structure and that you can access its properties with type safety.

TypeScript

```typescript
export interface Product {
  id: number;
  name: string;
  price: number;
}

export interface CartState {
  products: Product[];
}
```

2. Use createAction with props for Type-Safe Actions

NgRx provides the createAction function to define actions. Use the props function to define the types of any payload properties associated with the action.

TypeScript

```typescript
import        {        createAction,       props       }       from
'@ngrx/store';

export const addProduct = createAction(
  '[Product List] Add Product',
  props<{ product: Product }>()
);
```

This ensures that when you dispatch the `addProduct` action, you provide a payload that matches the `Product` type.

3. Type Your Reducers

Specify the types of the state and action parameters in your reducer functions. This helps TypeScript verify that your reducer logic is consistent with the defined types and that you're returning the correct state type.

TypeScript

```typescript
import { createReducer, on } from '@ngrx/store';
import { addProduct } from './cart.actions';

const initialState: CartState = {
  products: []
};

export const cartReducer = createReducer(
  initialState,
    on(addProduct, (state, { product }) => ({
...state, products: [...state.products, product]
}))
);
```

4. Create Type-Safe Selectors

Use `createSelector` to create selectors that are not only efficient but also type-safe. Specify the types of the state and any input parameters, as well as the return type of the selector.

TypeScript

```typescript
import { createSelector, createFeatureSelector }
from '@ngrx/store';
import { CartState } from './cart.reducer';

export const selectCartState =
createFeatureSelector<CartState>('cart');

export const selectCartProducts[1] =
createSelector(
  selectCartState,
  (state: CartState) => state.products
);
```

5. Leverage TypeScript Features

Generics: Use generics to create reusable reducers, effects, and selectors that can work with different state and action types.

Conditional Types: Use conditional types to define complex type relationships and constraints in your NgRx code.

Type Aliases: Create type aliases to simplify complex type definitions and improve code readability.

Benefits of Type-Safe NgRx

Early Error Detection: TypeScript catches type errors during development, preventing runtime surprises and reducing debugging time.

Improved Code Readability: Clear type annotations make your NgRx code easier to understand and maintain.

Enhanced Developer Experience: Your IDE can provide better code completion and suggestions with strong typing.

Increased Confidence: Type safety gives you more confidence in your code, knowing that your state management is robust and predictable.

By embracing TypeScript's type system and utilizing its features effectively, you can build NgRx applications that are not only type-safe but also more maintainable, scalable, and reliable.

6.3 Advanced NgRx patterns with TypeScript

Advanced NgRx Patterns with TypeScript

1. Creating Feature Stores

As your application grows, it's essential to organize your state into manageable units. Feature stores allow you to modularize your state, keeping related state and logic together.

Benefits:

Improved code organization and maintainability.

Reduced complexity in large applications.

Easier to reason about and test individual features.

Implementation:

Create separate reducers, actions, and selectors for each feature.

Use `createFeatureSelector` to create a selector for the feature state.

Compose selectors to access specific data within the feature state.

2. Entity State Adapter

The `EntityStateAdapter` provides a set of helper functions for managing collections of entities in your state. It simplifies common operations like adding, updating, and removing entities.

Benefits:

Reduced boilerplate code for entity management.

Improved performance with normalized state structure.

Simplified state updates with pre-built functions.

Implementation:

Create an adapter using `createEntityAdapter`.

Use adapter functions like `addOne`, `updateOne`, and `removeOne` in your reducers.

Use selectors provided by the adapter to access entity data.

3. Effects for Side Effects

Effects handle side effects, such as API calls, in your NgRx application. They listen for specific actions and perform asynchronous operations, then dispatch new actions to update the state based on the results.

Benefits:

Keeps your reducers pure and focused on state updates.

Centralizes side effect logic for easier management.

Improves testability by isolating side effects.

Implementation:

Create an injectable class decorated with `@Injectable`.

Use `createEffect` to define an effect that listens for an action.

Perform asynchronous operations within the effect.

Dispatch new actions to update the state based on the results.

4. Advanced Selectors

NgRx selectors can be combined and transformed to create powerful and reusable selectors.

Benefits:

Efficiently derive data from the state.

Reduce code duplication by reusing selectors.

Improve performance with memoized selectors.

Implementation:

Use `createSelector` to compose selectors.

Use selector operators like `map`, `filter`, and `reduce` to transform selected data.

Use `createSelectorFactory` to create parameterized selectors.

5. Strict Typing with TypeScript

TypeScript plays a crucial role in making your NgRx code type-safe and maintainable.

Benefits:

Catches type errors early during development.

Improves code readability and maintainability.

Enhances developer experience with better code completion and refactoring support.

Implementation:

Define interfaces or types for your state, actions, and payloads.

Use strong typing for reducers, effects, and selectors.

Leverage TypeScript features like generics and conditional types for advanced type safety.

By mastering these advanced NgRx patterns and leveraging TypeScript's type system, you can build highly robust, maintainable, and scalable Angular applications with efficient state management.

Chapter 7

Testing Angular Applications with TypeScript

7.1 Unit testing components, services, and directives

You're spot on! Unit testing is a crucial practice in software development, and Angular provides a robust testing framework to make it easier. Let's explore how to effectively unit test components, services, and directives in Angular.

Unit Testing in Angular

Unit tests focus on isolating individual units of code (components, services, directives, etc.) and verifying that they function correctly in isolation. This helps catch bugs early, ensures code quality, and makes refactoring safer.

1. Setting Up the Testing Environment

Angular projects come with built-in testing tools like Karma (test runner) and Jasmine (testing framework). You'll often use libraries like `@angular/core/testing` and `@angular/common/http/testing` to help with testing components and services that interact with Angular's core features or make HTTP requests.

2. Testing Components

When testing components, you'll typically:

Create a test bed: Use `TestBed` to configure a testing module that includes your component and its dependencies.

Create a component fixture: Use `createComponent` to create an instance of your component within the test bed.

Access the component instance and DOM: Use `fixture.componentInstance` and `fixture.nativeElement` to interact with your component and its DOM elements.

Trigger change detection: Use `fixture.detectChanges()` to update the component's view after making changes.

Make assertions: Use Jasmine's `expect` function to verify that the component behaves as expected.

Example:

TypeScript

```
import { ComponentFixture, TestBed } from
'@angular/core/testing';
import { By } from '@angular/platform-browser';
import { MyComponent¹ } from './my.component';

describe('MyComponent', () => {
  let component: MyComponent;
  let fixture: ComponentFixture<MyComponent>;

  beforeEach(async () => {
    await² TestBed.configureTestingModule({
      declarations: [ MyComponent³ ]
    })
    .compileComponents();

                        fixture          =
TestBed.createComponent(MyComponent);
```

```
  component = fixture.componentInstance;
  fixture.detectChanges();
});

it('should create', () => {
  expect(component).toBeTruthy();
});

it('should[4] display the title', () => {
              const      titleElement[5]     =
fixture.nativeElement.querySelector('h1');

expect(titleElement.textContent).toContain('My
Component');
});

  it('should increment the counter on button
click', () => {
              const      button      =
fixture.debugElement.query(By.css('button'));
  button.triggerEventHandler('click', null);
  fixture.detectChanges();[6]
              const      counterElement      =
fixture.nativeElement.querySelector('p');

expect(counterElement.textContent).toContain('Cou
nter: 1');
});
});
```

3. Testing Services

Testing services is usually straightforward since they don't involve
DOM interaction.

Create an instance of the service: Inject any dependencies the service needs.

Call the service's methods.

Make assertions to verify the results.

Example:

TypeScript

```typescript
import { TestBed } from '@angular/core/testing';
import { MyService } from './my.service';

describe('MyService', () => {
  let service: MyService;

  beforeEach(()⁷ => {
    TestBed.configureTestingModule({});
    service = TestBed.inject(MyService);
  });

  it('should be created', () => {
    expect(service).toBeTruthy();
  });

  it('should return⁸ the correct data', () => {
    const data = service.getData();
    expect(data).toEqual({ name: 'Test Data' });
  });
});
```

4. Testing Directives

Testing directives involves creating a host component that uses the directive and then testing the behavior of the directive within the context of that component.

Create a host component: A simple component that uses the directive.

Create a test bed with the host component and directive.

Access the directive: Use `fixture.debugElement.query(By.directive(MyDirective))` to get a reference to the directive.

Make assertions: Verify that the directive modifies the host element as expected.

Example:

TypeScript

```
import { Component, Directive, HostListener }
from '@angular/core';
import { ComponentFixture, TestBed } from
'@angular/core/testing';
import { By } from '@angular/platform-browser';[9]

@Directive({
  selector: '[appHighlight]'
})
export class HighlightDirective {
  @HostListener('mouseenter') onMouseEnter() {
    this.highlight('yellow');
  }

  @HostListener('mouseleave') onMouseLeave() {
    this.highlight(null);[10]
  }
```

```
  private highlight(color: string[11] | null) {
    // ... logic to highlight the element ...
  }
}

@Component({
  template: `<p appHighlight>Highlight me!</p>`
})
export class TestHostComponent {}

describe('HighlightDirective', () => {
                          let            fixture:
ComponentFixture<TestHostComponent>;

  beforeEach(async () => {
    await TestBed.configureTestingModule({
            declarations: [ HighlightDirective,
TestHostComponent ]
    })
    .compileComponents();

                              fixture        =
TestBed.createComponent(TestHostComponent);
    fixture.detectChanges();
  });

    it('should  highlight  the  element  on
mouseenter', () => {
                    const    element    =
fixture.debugElement.query(By.css('p')).nativeEle
ment;
    // Trigger the mouseenter event
                    element.dispatchEvent(new
MouseEvent('mouseenter'));
```

```
  // ... assertions to check if the element is
highlighted ...
  });
});
```

Key Considerations

Focus on isolated units: Test one unit at a time, mocking or stubbing dependencies.

Test different scenarios: Cover edge cases and various input values.

Keep tests concise and focused: Each test should have a clear purpose.

Use descriptive test names: Clearly indicate what is being tested.

By incorporating unit tests into your Angular development workflow, you can significantly improve code quality, reduce bugs, and make your applications more robust and maintainable.

7.2 End-to-end testing with Protractor and Cypress

You're moving into the realm of testing complete user flows! End-to-end (E2E) testing is critical for ensuring that all parts of your Angular application work together as expected. Protractor and Cypress are popular tools for E2E testing, each with its own strengths. Let's explore them:

End-to-End Testing with Protractor and Cypress

E2E tests simulate real user interactions with your application, navigating through pages, clicking buttons, filling out forms, and verifying that the application behaves correctly.

Protractor

Protractor was specifically designed for Angular applications. It interacts with your application through a real browser, simulating user actions and asserting on the results.

Key Features:

Built specifically for Angular: Understands Angular's structure and provides specialized locators.

WebDriverJS based: Leverages the power of Selenium WebDriver for browser automation.

Jasmine framework: Uses Jasmine for writing test specifications.

Example:

TypeScript

```typescript
// spec.ts
describe('Protractor Demo App', function() {
  it('should have a title', function() {

browser.get('http://juliemr.github.io/protractor-demo/');

        expect(browser.getTitle()).toEqual('Super Calculator');[1]
  });

  it('should add one and two', function() {

browser.get('http://juliemr.github.io/protractor-demo/');
    element(by.model('first')).sendKeys(1);
    element(by.model('second')).sendKeys(2);[2]
```

```
    element(by.id('gobutton')).click();


expect(element(by.binding('latest')).getText()).
        toEqual('3');
  });
});

// conf.js³
exports.config = {
  framework: 'jasmine',
                                seleniumAddress:
'http://localhost:4444/wd/hub',
  specs: ['spec.ts'],
  capabilities: {
    browserName: 'chrome'
  }
}
```

Cypress

Cypress is a more modern E2E testing framework known for its speed, ease of use, and powerful debugging capabilities.

Key Features:

Fast and reliable: Runs tests directly in the browser, providing faster execution and more consistent results.

Time-travel debugging: Allows you to "step back in time" to see what happened at each step of your tests.

Automatic waiting: Cypress automatically waits for elements to become visible and interactable, reducing the need for explicit waits.

Example:

JavaScript

```
// integration/spec.js
describe('Cypress Demo App', () => {
  it('should visit the page', () => {

cy.visit('http://juliemr.github.io/protractor-demo/');
  });

  it('should have a title', () => {
    cy.title().should('eq', 'Super Calculator');
  });

  it('should add one and two', () => {
    cy.get('[ng-model="first"]').type('1');
    cy.get('[ng-model="second"]').type('2');
    cy.get('#gobutton').click();

cy.get('[ng-binding="latest"]').should('have.text', '3');
  });
});
```

Choosing Between Protractor and Cypress

While Protractor was the default choice for Angular applications for a long time, Cypress has gained significant popularity due to its developer-friendly features and performance.

Consider **Protractor** if:

You have existing Protractor tests and don't want to migrate.

You need extensive cross-browser compatibility.

Consider **Cypress** if:

You're starting a new project or are willing to migrate.

You prioritize speed, ease of use, and debugging capabilities.

Key Considerations for E2E Testing

Test real user scenarios: Focus on testing critical user flows and interactions.

Keep tests independent: Each test should be able to run in isolation.

Use clear and descriptive test names: Make it easy to understand what each test is verifying.

Maintain a balance: E2E tests are valuable, but they can be slower to run. Balance them with unit tests for comprehensive coverage.

By incorporating E2E tests with Protractor or Cypress into your testing strategy, you can increase confidence in your Angular application's functionality and ensure a positive user experience.

7.3 Writing effective and type-safe tests

You're right to emphasize the importance of effective and type-safe tests! Let's break down the key principles and techniques for writing tests in Angular that are both robust and maintainable.

Writing Effective and Type-Safe Tests

1. Focus on Isolated Units

Unit tests should focus on testing individual units of code (components, services, directives, etc.) in isolation. This means mocking or stubbing their dependencies to ensure that you're testing the unit's logic and not the behavior of its dependencies.

Mocking: Create mock objects that simulate the behavior of real dependencies.

Stubbing: Provide simplified implementations of dependencies that return pre-defined values.

Example:

TypeScript

```typescript
// Mocking a service dependency in a component test
TestBed.configureTestingModule({
  providers: [
    { provide: MyService, useValue: { getData: ()
=> of({ name: 'Mocked Data' }) } }
  ]
});
```

2. Test Different Scenarios

Aim for comprehensive test coverage by testing different scenarios and edge cases. Consider various input values, error conditions, and user interactions to ensure your code behaves correctly under different circumstances.

Example:

TypeScript

```typescript
it('should handle valid input', () => {
  // ... test with valid input ...
});

it('should handle invalid input', () => {
  // ... test with invalid input ...
});

it('should handle error conditions', () => {
    // ... test with error responses from
dependencies ...
});
```

3. Keep Tests Concise and Focused

Each test should have a clear and specific purpose. Avoid testing multiple things in a single test. This makes it easier to identify the source of a failure and keeps your tests maintainable.

4. Use Descriptive Test Names

Use descriptive test names that clearly indicate what is being tested. This improves the readability of your tests and makes it easier to understand their purpose.

Example:

TypeScript

```typescript
it('should display the user\'s name', () => {
  // ... test logic ...
});
```

```
it('should update the counter on button click',
() => {
  // ... test logic ...
});
```

5. Leverage TypeScript's Type System

TypeScript's type system can help you write more robust and reliable tests.

Type Annotations: Use type annotations for variables, function parameters, and return values to ensure type safety in your tests.

Interfaces and Classes: Define interfaces and classes to represent test data and mock objects, ensuring consistency and type safety.

Generics: Use generics to write more flexible and reusable test code.

Example:

TypeScript

```
interface User {
  name: string;
  age: number;
}

it('should return a User object', () => {
  const data: User = service.getUser();
  expect(data).toEqual({ name: 'Test User', age:
30 });
});
```

6. Use a Testing Framework

Angular's testing framework, along with Jasmine, provides helpful utilities for writing and running tests.

`TestBed`: Configure a testing module for your components.

`ComponentFixture`: Interact with your component and its DOM.

`async` **and** `fakeAsync`: Test asynchronous code.

Jasmine's `expect`: Make assertions about your code's behavior.

7. Write Tests First (Test-Driven Development)

Consider adopting a test-driven development (TDD) approach, where you write tests before writing the actual code. This helps you clarify requirements, design better code, and ensure that your code works as expected from the start.

By following these principles and utilizing TypeScript's type safety, you can write effective and maintainable tests that improve the quality and reliability of your Angular applications.

Chapter 8

Performance Optimization and TypeScript

8.1 Identifying performance bottlenecks in Angular applications

Identifying Performance Bottlenecks in Angular Applications

Angular applications, especially complex ones, can sometimes suffer from performance issues. These issues can manifest as slow loading times, sluggish interactions, or excessive resource consumption. Identifying the root cause of these problems is the first step towards optimization.

1. Change Detection Overheads

Angular's change detection mechanism, while powerful, can become a bottleneck if not managed efficiently. Every time a change occurs in your application (user input, API response, timer events, etc.), Angular runs change detection to update the view. If your application has a large number of components or complex data bindings, this process can become expensive.

Identification:

Use the Angular profiler or browser developer tools to monitor the frequency and duration of change detection cycles.

Look for components that trigger change detection excessively or take a long time to process.

Pay attention to deeply nested component trees and complex data bindings.

2. Unnecessary Re-renders

Components might re-render even when their data hasn't changed. This can happen due to unnecessary change detection triggers or inefficient change detection strategies.

Identification:

Use `ChangeDetectionStrategy.OnPush` to optimize change detection and reduce unnecessary re-renders.

Avoid triggering change detection manually unless absolutely necessary.

Use immutable data structures to help Angular detect changes more efficiently.

3. Large Bundles and Long Loading Times

Large JavaScript bundles can significantly increase the initial load time of your application. This can be caused by including unnecessary libraries, not utilizing lazy loading, or inefficient build configurations.

Identification:

Analyze your bundle size using tools like Webpack Bundle Analyzer.

Identify large libraries or modules that can be lazy-loaded.

Optimize your build process to minimize bundle sizes.

4. Memory Leaks

Memory leaks occur when your application fails to release memory that is no longer needed. This can lead to gradual performance degradation and eventually crashes.

Identification:

Use browser developer tools to monitor memory usage over time.

Look for patterns of increasing memory consumption that don't correspond to actual application usage.

Pay attention to subscriptions and event listeners that are not properly unsubscribed.

5. DOM Manipulation Inefficiencies

Excessive or inefficient DOM manipulation can lead to performance issues, especially when dealing with large lists or complex animations.

Identification:

Use browser developer tools to profile JavaScript execution and identify DOM manipulation bottlenecks.

Optimize your templates to minimize DOM elements and bindings.

Use techniques like virtualization or pagination for large lists.

6. Network Requests

Slow or frequent network requests can impact application performance.

Identification:

Use browser developer tools to monitor network activity.

Identify slow or unnecessary requests.

Optimize API calls by reducing data transfer, using caching, and implementing efficient pagination.

Tools for Identifying Bottlenecks

Angular Profiler: Provides insights into change detection performance.

Browser Developer Tools: Offers profiling, network monitoring, and memory analysis capabilities.

Lighthouse: Audits your application and provides performance improvement suggestions.

WebPageTest: Analyzes your website's performance under different conditions.

By understanding these common performance bottlenecks and utilizing the appropriate tools, you can identify and address performance issues in your Angular applications, leading to a faster and more responsive user experience.

8.2 Using TypeScript to improve code efficiency and maintainability

Improving Code Efficiency

Early Error Detection: TypeScript's static typing allows the compiler to catch type-related errors during development, preventing runtime errors and reducing debugging time. This leads to faster development cycles and more robust applications.

Improved Code Optimization: TypeScript's type information enables the compiler to perform better code optimizations, resulting in smaller and more efficient JavaScript bundles. This can lead to faster loading times and improved performance.

Enhanced Code Readability: TypeScript's type annotations and interfaces make code more self-documenting and easier to understand. This improves developer productivity and reduces the time spent deciphering code.

Refactoring with Confidence: TypeScript's compiler helps identify potential issues caused by code refactoring, making it safer and less error-prone to make changes to your codebase.

Improving Code Maintainability

Clearer Code Structure: TypeScript's features like interfaces, classes, and enums encourage a more structured and organized codebase. This makes it easier to understand, navigate, and maintain the code, especially in large projects.

Reduced Code Duplication: TypeScript's support for generics and modules promotes code reuse and reduces code duplication. This leads to a more concise and maintainable codebase.

Better Collaboration: TypeScript's type safety and code clarity improve collaboration among developers. With clear type definitions, it's easier for developers to understand each other's code and work together effectively.

Long-Term Maintainability: TypeScript's focus on type safety and code structure makes it easier to maintain applications over the long term. As your application grows and evolves, TypeScript helps ensure that the code remains consistent and manageable.

Specific Examples

Interfaces: Defining interfaces for data models ensures that data is consistently structured throughout your application, reducing errors and improving maintainability.

Generics: Creating reusable components and services with generics reduces code duplication and improves type safety.

Enums: Using enums for predefined values improves code readability and prevents errors caused by typos or incorrect values.

Access Modifiers: Using access modifiers (`public`, `private`, `protected`) helps encapsulate code and prevent unintended modifications, improving maintainability.

8.3 Advanced techniques: ahead-of-time (AOT) compilation, lazy loading

You're diving into some powerful optimization techniques! Ahead-of-Time (AOT) compilation and lazy loading are key strategies for improving the performance of Angular applications, especially as they grow in size and complexity. Let's explore how these techniques work and how they benefit your applications.

Advanced Techniques: AOT Compilation and Lazy Loading

Ahead-of-Time (AOT) Compilation

AOT compilation is a process where Angular compiles your application's HTML and TypeScript code into highly optimized JavaScript code *before* the browser downloads and runs it. This contrasts with Just-in-Time (JIT) compilation, where the browser compiles the code at runtime.

Benefits of AOT Compilation

Faster Rendering: AOT compilation eliminates the need for the browser to compile the application at runtime, resulting in significantly faster rendering times and improved initial load performance.

Smaller Bundle Sizes: AOT compilation removes the Angular compiler from the bundle, reducing the overall size of the JavaScript files that need to be downloaded. This leads to faster download times and improved performance, especially on mobile devices or slower connections.

Early Error Detection: AOT compilation can detect template binding errors during the build process, allowing you to catch and fix issues before they reach production.

Improved Security: AOT compilation can help improve security by reducing the amount of code that needs to be executed at runtime, making it more difficult for attackers to inject malicious code.

How to Enable AOT Compilation

In your Angular project, you can enable AOT compilation by setting the `aot` option to `true` in the `angular.json` configuration file. The Angular CLI handles the AOT compilation process during the build.

Lazy Loading

Lazy loading is a technique where you split your application into smaller modules that are loaded on demand, only when they are needed. This can significantly improve the initial load time of your application, as the browser only needs to download the code necessary for the initial view.

Benefits of Lazy Loading

Faster Initial Load: By only loading the essential code upfront, lazy loading reduces the initial bundle size and improves the time it takes for the application to become interactive.

Improved Performance: Lazy loading can improve overall performance by reducing the amount of code that needs to be parsed and executed, especially for large applications.

Resource Optimization: Lazy loading helps conserve resources by only loading modules when they are required, reducing memory consumption and improving performance on low-powered devices.

How to Implement Lazy Loading

In Angular, you can implement lazy loading using the `loadChildren` property in your route configuration. This property specifies the path to the module that should be lazy-loaded.

TypeScript

```
const routes: Routes = [
  {
    path: 'dashboard',
                    loadChildren:        ()      =>
import('./dashboard/dashboard.module').then(m   =>
m.DashboardModule)
  }
];
```

Combining AOT and Lazy Loading

AOT compilation and lazy loading work together to optimize
Angular application performance. AOT compilation ensures that
the lazy-loaded modules are also compiled ahead of time,
maximizing performance benefits.

By implementing these advanced techniques, you can significantly
improve the performance of your Angular applications, resulting in
faster loading times, smoother interactions, and a better user
experience.

Chapter 9

Building and Deploying with TypeScript

9.1 Optimizing the build process for production

Optimizing the Angular Build Process for Production

The Angular CLI provides a powerful build process, but there are several ways to fine-tune it for production deployments:

1. Ahead-of-Time (AOT) Compilation

As we discussed earlier, AOT compilation is crucial for production builds. It pre-compiles your application's templates and code, resulting in:

Faster rendering in the browser.

Smaller bundle sizes.

Early error detection.

Improved security.

2. Production Flag

When you build your Angular application with the `--prod` flag (or `ng build --configuration production`), the CLI automatically applies a set of production optimizations, including:

AOT compilation

Bundling and minification of code

Tree-shaking (removing unused code)

Dead code elimination

3. Bundling and Minification

Bundling combines your application's JavaScript files into a single file (or a few smaller chunks), reducing the number of network requests needed to load the application. Minification removes unnecessary characters (whitespace, comments, etc.) from your code, further reducing file sizes.

Tools: Angular CLI uses Webpack for bundling and Terser for minification.

4. Tree-Shaking

Tree-shaking eliminates unused code from your application's bundles. This is especially important when using third-party libraries, as you often don't need all the code they provide.

How it works: Modern JavaScript module systems (like ES modules) allow for static analysis of code, enabling tree-shaking to identify and remove unused exports.

5. Lazy Loading

Lazy loading splits your application into smaller modules that are loaded on demand. This can significantly improve initial load time and reduce resource consumption.

Implementation: Use the `loadChildren` property in your route configuration to specify lazy-loaded modules.

6. Optimizing Assets

Optimize your images, fonts, and other assets to reduce their file sizes.

Techniques:

Image compression

Using web fonts efficiently

Caching static assets

7. Caching

Implement caching strategies to store static assets and API responses, reducing the number of network requests and improving load times.

Service Workers: Use service workers to cache assets and enable offline functionality.

HTTP caching headers: Configure your server to send appropriate caching headers.

8. Monitoring and Analysis

Continuously monitor your application's performance using tools like:

Lighthouse: Provides audits and suggestions for performance improvement.

Browser Developer Tools: Offers performance profiling and network analysis.

WebPageTest: Analyzes your website's performance under different conditions.

9. Build Configuration

Fine-tune your build configuration in the `angular.json` file to optimize for specific needs. You can customize settings for AOT compilation, bundling, output paths, and more.

By implementing these optimization strategies and continuously monitoring your application's performance, you can ensure that your Angular builds are production-ready, providing a fast and efficient user experience.

9.2 Deployment strategies for Angular applications

You're thinking about the final step! Deploying your Angular application effectively is crucial for making it accessible to users. Let's explore some common deployment strategies:

1. Traditional Web Hosting

This is a straightforward approach where you build your Angular application and upload the production-ready files to a web server.

Process:

Use the Angular CLI to build your application with the `--prod` flag (`ng build --configuration production`).

Upload the contents of the `dist` folder to your web server (using FTP, SSH, or other methods).

Configure your web server (Apache, Nginx) to serve the `index.html` file as the entry point.

Suitable for:

Simple applications

Situations where you have existing web hosting infrastructure

2. Cloud Platforms

Cloud platforms offer scalable and reliable infrastructure for deploying Angular applications.

Popular options:

Netlify: Simplifies deployment with continuous deployment features.

Vercel: Offers serverless functions and edge caching for optimal performance.

Firebase Hosting: Provides fast and secure hosting with easy integration with other Firebase services.

AWS Amplify: Offers a full suite of tools for building and deploying web applications.

Azure Static Web Apps: Provides streamlined deployment for static websites with serverless API support.

Benefits:

Scalability

Reliability

Easy setup and deployment

Integration with other cloud services

3. Server-Side Rendering (SSR)

SSR renders your Angular application on the server, sending a fully rendered page to the client. This can improve SEO and initial load performance.

Angular Universal: Angular's SSR solution.

Benefits:

Improved SEO

Faster initial load time

Better performance on low-powered devices

Considerations:

Increased server-side load

More complex setup

4. Serverless Functions

Serverless functions allow you to run your Angular application as a set of functions triggered by events. This can be a cost-effective and scalable solution.

Platforms: AWS Lambda, Azure Functions, Google Cloud Functions

Benefits:

Cost-effectiveness

Scalability

Reduced operational overhead

Considerations:

Potential cold starts (initial latency)

Vendor lock-in

5. Docker Containers

Docker containers package your Angular application and its dependencies into a portable unit that can be easily deployed to various environments.

Benefits:

Consistency across environments

Portability

Scalability

Considerations:

Learning curve for Docker

Container orchestration for complex deployments

Choosing a Deployment Strategy

The best deployment strategy depends on your application's specific needs and your infrastructure. Consider factors like:

Application complexity

Scalability requirements

Performance needs

Budget

Existing infrastructure

By carefully evaluating these factors and choosing the appropriate deployment strategy, you can ensure that your Angular application is accessible, performant, and scalable.

9.3 TypeScript in the cloud: server-side rendering (SSR) and serverless functions

You're exploring the exciting intersection of TypeScript, cloud computing, and modern web development! Both Server-Side Rendering (SSR) and serverless functions offer powerful ways to enhance Angular applications, and TypeScript plays a crucial role in ensuring type safety and maintainability in these environments. Let's dive in:

TypeScript in the Cloud

TypeScript's benefits, such as static typing, code clarity, and improved tooling, extend seamlessly to cloud-based Angular applications. Whether you're using SSR or serverless functions, TypeScript helps you write more robust, maintainable, and scalable code.

Server-Side Rendering (SSR) with TypeScript

SSR involves rendering your Angular application on the server, sending a fully rendered HTML page to the client. This can improve SEO, perceived performance, and the experience for users with slower devices or connections.

Angular Universal: Angular's SSR solution, Angular Universal, works seamlessly with TypeScript. You can write your server-side rendering logic in TypeScript, taking advantage of type safety and code completion.

Type Safety: TypeScript ensures that your data models and components are consistent between the server and client, reducing errors and improving maintainability.

Code Sharing: TypeScript allows you to share code between the server and client, promoting code reuse and reducing duplication.

Serverless Functions with TypeScript

Serverless functions let you run parts of your Angular application as independent functions in the cloud, triggered by events. This can be a cost-effective and scalable way to handle specific tasks or microservices.

TypeScript Support: Popular serverless platforms like AWS Lambda, Azure Functions, and Google Cloud Functions all have excellent support for TypeScript.

Type-Safe APIs: You can define type-safe interfaces for your serverless function inputs and outputs, ensuring data integrity and reducing errors.

Improved Code Organization: TypeScript's module system helps you organize your serverless functions and their dependencies, improving code maintainability.

Example: Serverless Function with TypeScript

TypeScript

```typescript
// api/users.ts
import { AzureFunction, Context, HttpRequest } from "@azure/functions"

const httpTrigger: AzureFunction = async function (context: Context, req:1 HttpRequest): Promise<void> {
  context.log('HTTP trigger function processed a request.');

  const2 users = [
    { id: 1, name: 'Alice' },
    { id: 2, name: 'Bob' }
  ];
```

```
context.res = {
  // status: 200, /* Defaults to 200 */
  body: users
};
};

export default httpTrigger;
```

Benefits of Using TypeScript in the Cloud

Improved Developer Productivity: TypeScript's code completion, navigation, and refactoring tools enhance developer productivity in cloud environments.

Reduced Errors: Static typing helps catch errors early in the development process, reducing debugging time and improving code quality.

Enhanced Maintainability: TypeScript's code clarity and structure make it easier to maintain and evolve cloud-based applications over time.

Scalability and Reliability: TypeScript's focus on type safety and code organization contributes to building more scalable and reliable cloud applications.

By combining the power of TypeScript with cloud technologies like SSR and serverless functions, you can create Angular applications that are not only performant and scalable but also robust, maintainable, and ready to meet the demands of modern web development.